10

Things You Might Need To Hear Today

SAM NELSON

(okay, so there's more than 10 things, but who's counting?)

a Hezzie Mae publication
Duluth, MN.
www.HezzieMae.com

ISBN: 979-8-9997402-7-4

I don't have an academic degree. I didn't study from a textbook. I learned it from living life.

I wrote this because once I understood it, I couldn't keep it to myself—I needed others to have the same opportunity.

This work is personal. It is embodied. And it is a living, ever-evolving body of research.

Sam

For my husband, Scott.

And for everyone who learned to ask,
"What's wrong with me?"

This is my offering to you.
Not advice. Not instructions. Just reminders.

"My biggest hope with this is that,
even if it's just one person out there,
they know they're not alone."

— Scott Nelson

The Cost

Capacity - Nervous System - Sensory

Just because someone looks okay
doesn't mean they feel okay.

We can't always see what they're
carrying.

It's not just you if you feel constantly behind on just about everything.

Trying to hold it all
together when things are
not okay is not easy.

You know what's toxic?

Being praised for pushing past your limits.

Being rewarded for ignoring your needs.

Being told you're "doing great" while you're
slowly disappearing to make things easier
for everyone else.

.

I've had multiple naps today.

I needed them.

I have a laundry list of things I want to do.
Should do. Have to do.

And sometimes I have to say, *"Too bad, not
happening right now."*

Especially when everything lands at once
and feels like too much. Sometimes the
bare minimum is all we're able to give.

That's not a failure. It's called being
human—with a nervous system and
fluctuating capacity.

Capitalism wants you to forget that. I'm
here to remind you: you are not a
machine.

If everything feels like a lot right now,
it's because it is a lot.

Be as gentle as you can with yourself.

"I was in a really, really low point, where
you hit burnout, and you can't mask
anymore. You feel like you're falling
apart. You don't know why, you think
you're terrible, and you suck.

And since you don't know there's
actually a biological thing happening.
You think it's you."

— Scott Nelson

My house is a mess. My car is a mess.
It can be overwhelming and
frustrating.

But it is not a moral failing.

What's hard for me might not be hard for you.

What's beyond your capacity today might not be beyond mine. Some things are consistently hard. Others depend on the day.

"But that's not hard for me."
"But you did it last time."

Both assume capacity is fixed. It's not.

"I can do it, so you should be able to" isn't helpful.

I am exhausted. That's it. That's the note.

Please be gentle with yourself if
you can't do what you were able to
do yesterday, or last week, or six
months ago.

Capacity isn't fixed. It changes.
Some days you can.
Some days you can't.

Different nervous systems.

Different thresholds.

All equally real.

"No wonder I had a full-blown meltdown
and never really recovered. How many years
did this build up before it finally overflowed,
and now I don't know what to do with it...
the mask got shattered, and I can't throw it
back on anymore."

— Scott Nelson

Tonight, my daughter had a meltdown.
Sometimes she gets stuck.

Tonight was a stuck night.

She wasn't trying to be difficult. She was having a hard time.

And my job in that moment wasn't discipline or control.

It was to offer support without turning her distress into a moral failure or shaming her.

Trying to stay regulated when your kid is having a hard time can be so challenging.

I sat in my car at home. Frozen. For an hour.

I couldn't get up.

My body had decided.

And that was that.

Capitalism: What have you done
today? Nothing. You're falling behind.
You should be doing more.

Nervous system: I am in survival mode.
I cannot do a lot right now. That is not
a personal failing. That is information
about my current state.

What if we saw dysregulation
as a nervous system state and
not a character trait?

Just a reminder that consistency is made
out to be some kind of virtue.

Something we should all be able to do.

And that if we don't, if we can't...we
have somehow failed.

But please don't believe the lie. This is
not how humans work. This is not how
bodies work. This isn't how nervous
systems work.

We don't all process the world the
same way.

For some of us, sights, sounds,
textures, and smells land gently.

For others, those same things can be
overwhelming, distracting, or even
painful.

None of it is wrong. It's simply
different—and those sensitivities can
even vary day to day.

For some people, background noise really does fade into the background. They can read, work, or have a conversation in a busy space without a second thought.

For others—like my husband—it's anything but background. It's distracting and exhausting, and it can build into unbearable overwhelm.

Meanwhile, I can be sitting right next to him, barely noticing it.

You can't learn to trust your
body's signals if someone else is
always overriding them.

Many neurodivergent people have never
had their internal experience named in a
way that matches what they actually felt.

Instead, they were told:
"You are overreacting."
"You are too sensitive."
"You are being dramatic."
"You are fine."

Over time, this creates masking, shutdown,
shame, and self-doubt. It pulls us away
from our own signals. Not because
something is wrong with us, but because
we were not understood or supported.

Brain imaging shows that autistic and
sensory-sensitive people process sound,
touch, and light through different
pathways in the brain.

That means sound, touch, and light can
register completely differently from
one person to another.

Forcing food when the smell, texture,
or taste feels "wrong" isn't just
uncomfortable—it can be distressing.

It's the same with clothing tags, certain
fabrics, or even lotions.

I have no problem putting on
sunscreen, but my husband absolutely
hates the feeling of it.

What soothes one person can feel
unbearable to another.

Both are valid.

Listening to your body can feel foreign.

Not because you don't have signals.
Because you were taught to ignore them
and then rewarded for it.

The override becomes automatic.
The disconnection feels normal.
And eventually it catches up to you.

Learning to listen to your body is not
indulgent. It is a repair with yourself.

Many of us have had our sensory experiences and emotional reactions dismissed.

When you grow up being told that what your body feels is wrong and that your emotions are too much, you learn to distrust yourself.

You learn to believe the problem is you.

'I don't know if other people hear it.
I hear it. I can hear the lights."

— Scott Nelson

Chewing gum is a form of stimming.

Chewing gum can help meet oral
sensory needs.

Chewing gum can be a simple form
of regulation.

My oldest daughter has always
chewed on things. I can't tell you how
many water bottles she's ruined.
Reusable plastic straws destroyed.
Disposable spoons mangled.

We stopped caring—and started
embracing it.

Maybe you were that kid.

Maybe you were told to stop
sensory seeking or stimming.

Maybe you learned to hide it—or
swap it for something more
"socially acceptable."

If that was you, I want you to
know there was never anything
wrong with you.

"The tag in my shirt is wrong."

— Scott Nelson

Because here's the truth:
pushing someone through
sensory overwhelm isn't helpful.

It can be traumatic.

You're overstimulated.
You're overwhelmed.
You're tired before you even get
out of the car.

You're carrying everyone's expectations.
You're trying to prevent meltdowns: your
kids and your own.

And you're trying not to disappoint anyone.

And you're supposed to do this all
while smiling?

"All the lights are off because
I'm just so overdone."

— Scott Nelson

Autistic and ADHD nervous systems often take longer to recover from overstimulation.

Please be gentle with yourself, your partner, or your child during this time.

Lights may need to be turned off.

Demands may need to be lowered.

Plans may need to be cancelled.

"I want to go. I'm overstimulated."

— My 9-year-old

Sensory overwhelm can trigger meltdowns or shutdowns—very real nervous system responses, not "tantrums" or "overreactions."

The body is saying: *this was too much.*

"I don't want to talk to anybody. I don't want anyone to ask me anything."

— Scott Nelson

I can be overstimulated and overdone,
and my child may need the very input
that is overstimulating me.

Neither one of us is wrong.
It's just a mismatch.

"My skin is crawling, and all I can think
about is how uncomfortable I am."

— Scott Nelson

I am so overstimulated right now.

Every little sound is amplified, and every demand being made of me feels intense.

I am at my max.

There are times when we need to...

Turn the sound down.

Turn off the lights.

Leave the room.

Communicate how we are feeling.

Put on headphones.

Go to the bathroom.

Ask for what we need.

Walk away.

Here's Why

Harm - Systems - Power

There can be a lot of power held
in the words we use.

They can trigger real
physiological responses.

The same part of the brain that
registers physical pain also
registers emotional pain.

Harm isn't always loud or extreme.

It's often mundane. It's often *normal*.
It's often socially acceptable.

And it's often invisible...except to the
person carrying it.

Words that incite toxic positivity
are harmful.

They sound like help.

But every single one sends the same
message:
Your pain is inconvenient.
Please package it differently.
I need you to be okay.

This is often less about helping the
person in distress and more about
managing the discomfort of the
person who has to witness it.

We often take what the environment tells us (explicitly or implicitly) about ourselves as truth.

Especially when we can't see the systems we're in and what they demand.

Especially when we don't have language for it.

Especially when everyone around us seems to be managing just fine.

A conversation a lot of people aren't ready for: harm doesn't help people learn, even when we call it necessary...even when we frame it "nicely."

"But they need to learn x" is often how distress, pressure, or force get justified.

The real question is: *learn what?*

And who does that learning actually benefit?

The way we treat children says a
lot about us as a society.

They are the most vulnerable in
our communities.

When harm is normalized as
necessary for children, it becomes
easier to justify that same harm,
and worse, everywhere else.

Context does not erase harm.

Understanding someone's behavior never negates the real impact their actions have on others.

Believe people when they show you
who they are.

Giving the benefit of the doubt makes
sense when there is confusion.

It does not make sense when there is a
clear, repeated refusal to listen about
ethics, humanity, or harm.

When harm is normalized long enough,
we stop asking whether it's harm.

I feel this.
I'm being told I shouldn't.
I don't know how to trust myself.

That's the harm. A person learning, over
and over, that their inner experience is
not credible.

That's epistemic injustice.
Your reality is dismissed and treated
as not real.

Epistemic Injustice: The existence of a distinctive type of injustice in which a wrong is done to someone specifically in their capacity as a knower.

Fricker, Miranda (2007). *Epistemic Injustice: Power and The Ethics of Knowing* (Oxford University Press).

Disbelief is an effective strategy for avoiding both personal and systemic change. It protects the status quo: environments stay the same, authority goes unquestioned, and the person not being believed is expected to carry the cost.

This is especially true for those whose internal experiences are rarely treated as credible—children, disabled and neurodivergent folks, and many people marginalized by race, gender, body size, language, and class.

Over time, when our feelings,
sensations, and experiences are
continually dismissed or minimized,
we start to question ourselves and
our own bodies.

We begin scanning our signals,
wondering if they can even be
trusted.

Most of us were not allowed to feel
our feelings growing up.

They were minimized, punished,
ignored, or made inconvenient.

So it makes sense that being around
someone who is fully expressing
themselves can be triggering.

That doesn't mean the feelings are the
problem. As long as everyone is safe,
feelings are not dangerous, even if they
are distressing.

What causes harm is making those
feelings wrong—rushing to stop them,
control them, or discipline them out
of existence.

The body doesn't stop responding.
It just stops being believed.

So we turn it inward.
We decide we are the problem.

Because that's the only explanation
we've ever been given.

When we train people to
override their discomfort,
suppress their questions, and
always obey, we are not just
creating well-behaved people.

We are creating people who
struggle to trust themselves.

We silence our own discomfort.

We override our own clarity.

We tell ourselves to stop making waves.

We comply before anyone even asks.

We no longer need something outside of us

to keep us "in line."

We do it to ourselves.

When your sensory world, emotional responses, attention, communication style, or regulation needs don't match what's considered *normal*, your experiences are more likely to be questioned, corrected, or dismissed.

Not once—but constantly.

Lived experience is a legitimate source
of knowledge.

Most of us have been taught to treat it
as less than other forms of knowing.
That's not by accident.

When we're taught not to trust
ourselves, we start looking outward for
permission. That's how authority stays
centered.

Neurodivergent kids, especially
those who are more direct,
more literal,
more curious,
or more likely to question
authority,
are more often punished.

In case no one told you today:
your lived experience is valid.

Your family may not believe you.
Your friends may not believe you.
Your doctor may not believe you.

You might not even believe you.

They may not intend it to be
harmful— but disbelief is harm.

Often, behavior that is inconvenient, not
preferred, or benign gets pathologized.

Even when no one is in danger.
Even when no harm is happening.

Even when it's simply uncomfortable for
someone else, or they don't understand it.

Are we more concerned about making
things more comfortable for the people
around them?

Or are we more concerned about the
person's internal experience and
well-being?

Uncomfortable is uncomfortable.
It's *not* nothing.

But discomfort and dismissal do
not carry the same cost. And
when we treat them like they do,
we trade temporary relief for
longer-lasting harm.

You don't have to agree with someone's internal experience to trust that it's real for them.

The hardest thing I ever had to
learn how to do...was trust myself.

As a society, we care a whole lot about people behaving in "appropriate" and in "socially acceptable" ways, and we don't really give a shit what it costs them.

We rarely ask about the harm it causes. About what gets suppressed, erased, or overridden in the process.

This is not accidental.

It is a systemic power play.

"You're lazy."

"You should do more."

"Other people manage this."

That voice isn't yours. It was installed by systems that needed you to override your own in the service of theirs.

This work is forged in grief.
In heartbreak.

In watching someone you deeply love
suffer because they see themselves as a
problem.

The shame that started outside them
insidiously crept in until they believed it
was them. Completely unaware of the
systems that create a culture where this
kind of harm is seen as normal and "just
how it is."

And this is not an isolated incident...so
many others feel this way.

Most systems, institutions, and
organizations measure success by
compliance and productivity.

What if we measured it by safety,
agency, and dignity?

Those are different measures—and
they lead to very different results.

Results centered on the person.
Not their performance.

Advocacy is intersectional.

Systems don't harm people in silos. The same systems criminalizing immigrants also police Black and Brown bodies, punish disability and neurodivergence, control gender and reproduction, and turn care into something that must be earned through paperwork and compliance.

People don't live one identity at a time. Harm doesn't either.

Solidarity is necessary.

Authoritarian systems survive by
teaching us to see harm as something
that happens to other people.

By whispering, *this isn't about you.*
By keeping empathy conditional and
solidarity delayed.

A regulated nervous system is
inconvenient for systems that
require compliance.

A person connected to their own
signals—who trusts their own
experience, who can feel when
something is wrong—is harder to
exploit.

What gets labeled as *defiance* in marginalized bodies often gets labeled as *leadership* in privileged ones.

In so many spaces, especially those with children, disabled people, or anyone with less power, discomfort is normalized as long as the task gets done.

The metric becomes completion, not consent: compliance, not safety.

The person is expected to adapt, so the environment doesn't have to. When comfort and efficiency matter more than consent, someone will pay for it.

And it is almost always the person with the least power in the room.

Caring for the most vulnerable
shouldn't be seen as radical...but
patriarchy makes it radical because
it's a real threat to its dominion.

We were rarely taught to question.

We weren't even allowed to question.

Not the adults.

Not the people in power.

Not the system.

Not the environment.

Because questioning would
disrupt the hierarchy.

Compliance is behavior that satisfies
someone else's criteria.

It doesn't ask: *Is this person okay?*

It doesn't ask: *What is the cost to the individual?*

It doesn't ask: *Who benefits from their compliance?*

It asks: *Are they doing what I need them to do?*

Most of us were trained into
compliance early.

Not just socially, but physiologically.
Our nervous systems learned that
resistance equals danger.

That questioning authority risks
punishment. That safety comes from
going along.

Because often, it did.

Compliance is not just ideological.
It is embodied.

You can't build a culture on
obedience and then be shocked when
it does what it's always done.

Over time, the body starts to associate
safety with compliance.

People learn to adjust themselves.
They mask differences.
They minimize needs.
They monitor behavior.

Not because they believe the system is
right, but because being fully themselves
has proven costly, time and time again.

That isn't a character flaw. It's what
happens when survival depends on
adaptation.

Not all compliance is harmful.
Sometimes it's needed for actual safety.

But unquestioned compliance?

That's where it gets dangerous.

This isn't about purity or
always getting it right.

It's about refusing to keep
participating in harmful systems
once we can see what's happening.

What Do We Do?

Reclamation - Care - Community

"Talking about this stuff has changed
my life. I still struggle, but overall, it's
changed my life so much."

— Scott Nelson

Disabled is not a bad word.

Disabled is not a bad word.

Disabled is not a bad word.

Regulation is not a moral achievement.

Dysregulation is data.

You don't have to be calm to be valid.

And sometimes, even with the best intentions, I'm not regulated.

None of us is all the time.

What I've learned is that shaming myself for those moments doesn't help.

You cannot shame yourself into regulation.
You cannot shame others into regulation.

Regulation requires safety, and shame is a
threat to our nervous system.

Dysregulation is still hard,
messy, and stressful.

But making someone feel bad
for struggling only adds another
layer of pain.

Women are powerful.

If we weren't there would be no
reason to try and control us.

Accommodation isn't lowering the bar.

It's adjusting the environment so participation is actually possible.

So often we pathologize what we don't
understand.

More understanding can help change that.

It can change how you see others.

And maybe more importantly, how you
see yourself.

What's considered normal is often simply what the system was built around and what we are used to.

You're allowed to disrupt that.

Your needs matter,

Your boundaries matter,

Your recovery matters,

And you don't owe anyone a version
of yourself that requires self-abandonment.

You don't owe anyone access to you.

I am allowed to disengage from conversations that are not rooted in mutual respect or genuine curiosity.

I don't owe continued access to people who repeatedly refuse both.

If this resonates, you're allowed to hold it too—at your own pace, and in whatever way is safest for you.

You have permission to leave the event
or social setting if it's too much for you.

"Before diagnosis, I would start magnifying how bad I felt about myself.

Now I actually know what it is, and I understand it.

I'm not so mad at myself. Yes, I'm super low, but the self-thoughts are different than before I was diagnosed. I'm not as hard on myself about it like I used to be."
— Scott Nelson

The older I get, the less I care what other people think of me.

I love it.

I am a people pleaser.
I did not get to practice
resistance as a kid.

If I am honest, my kids are way
better at it than I am.

It has taken a lot of small steps
for me to even get here. Because
compliance has often felt safer.

Sensory differences are not problems to fix.

Lack of eye contact is not something to increase.

Meltdowns are not something to shame.

This is your reminder: Don't pressure anyone, kids or adults, to eat foods they don't want.

And if someone can't advocate for themselves, step in.

Food is not a performance. It's not a moral issue. No one owes tasting, trying, or pretending.

I truly do not care if my kids ever try a
bite of green bean casserole.

What I do care about is that they grow
up knowing their "no" actually matters.

That their bodies are allowed to be
inconvenient.

Safe foods are often processed foods or fast food because they are consistent.

It's a sensory experience that is predictable in a very unpredictable world.

So often, a lack of understanding labels people as "picky eaters," and it does nothing to try to understand why people like or dislike certain things.

We end up forcing people to eat things that are sensory hell for them.

Trust grows when boundaries
are honored, not pushed.

Morality belongs to harm, consent violations, coercion, exploitation, abuse of power—not to stimming, tone, eye contact, speed, stillness, or harmless difference.

You don't owe anyone a hug.

If "no" comes with shame, teasing,
guilt, or fear, it is not a real choice.

It is compliance, not consent.

Consent is radical in a culture that
doesn't ask for permission.

We're rarely taught how to
practice consent with ourselves.

Culture trains us to attend,
comply, and push through.

Sometimes reclaiming consent
looks as simple and as radical as
saying, *"I don't actually want to go
to that social event."*

Stop saying, *"Try harder."*

Start asking,
"What might support look like for you?"

And then actually listen to people.
Support is different for everyone.

You don't age out of needing care,
boundaries, support, and
accommodations.

Needs change.
They fluctuate.
They don't disappear.

Needing support is not something
you outgrow.

Relying on support is not a moral deficit.

Needing each other is not a weakness.

It is deeply human. Many of us were taught that needing help makes us less valuable. Many of us were taught that being tired from caregiving makes us selfish.

Both of those narratives can be harmful. We can honor support needs and honor caregiver capacity at the same time.

Real support should increase safety, agency, and access.

It shouldn't require someone to make themselves smaller, quieter, or easier to manage.

So it's worth asking: *who is this actually for?*

The person receiving it, or the system that wants things quieter, faster, and easier to manage?

Needs aren't a problem.

The problem is being told that
you shouldn't have them.

The problem is being punished
or shamed for them.

The problem is being
denied support.

Let's make it safe for our kids to question us.

Let's be willing to admit when we're wrong.

Let's embrace critical thinking.

It starts with us.

Children learn how to treat themselves by
watching how we treat them.

They learn whether their limits are respected.
Whether their signals are believed.
Whether they are allowed to take up space
as they are.

We can't ask children to honor their limits
if we don't model what that looks like.

If I say, "*Listen to your body*," but then
override theirs because it's inconvenient—
what am I teaching?

A child raised to trust their own experience, know their needs are legitimate, and not comply out of fear often becomes an adult who is harder to exploit.

That's not permissive parenting.

That's a direct threat to the current social power system. And the system knows it. If it wasn't a threat, it wouldn't have to make those things feel wrong.

Parenting to cultivate these traits is resistance.

If your child says something is

too loud,

too itchy,

too overwhelming,

too bright,

or too much.

Please believe them.
Advocacy starts with trusting
their experience, even when
others dismiss it or don't
understand it.

Children who are overwhelmed and
having a meltdown deserve support.

Adults who are overwhelmed and
having a meltdown deserve support.

When you are overwhelmed and having
a meltdown, you deserve support.

Autistic children grow up to be autistic adults. Support needs don't vanish with age—they shift.

The world needs to remember that.

When kids learn that their "no" leads to disconnection, they do not learn curiosity.

They learn: *"My body's signals are less important than other people's expectations."*

When we train children to mask, to be quieter, stiller, easier to manage, we need to ask:

Who is this actually for?

Whom does this benefit?

Who does this cost?

Because there is always a cost, either the child pays it by masking more, accumulating shame, and learning that who they are is the problem.

Or the adults around them pay it by making accommodations, changing the environment, being a steward of their power, and taking on an ethical responsibility. Those are not equivalent costs. Someone always pays.

I don't think we realize just how big a deal
it is to believe children when they tell us
what they're experiencing instead of
dismissing them when they say, "*this is too
hot, too bright, too itchy, too much.*"

We are teaching them that their perception
is real and worth taking seriously.

Believing them doesn't mean they always get
what they want or never do hard things; it
means we stop telling their bodies they're
wrong in the process.

We are all learning.

We will all make mistakes.

Repair matters more than our ego.

Let us be stewards of our power.

We are creatures of connection, and
not being believed can feel unbearable,
which is why there is something so
powerful about truly being seen by
someone.

This is your gentle nudge to remember
that spending time on your special
interests is part of caring for yourself.

People just want to be seen, even if
nothing can be changed.

Being seen signals safety.

"We definitely don't have our stuff figured out. We're still muddling through everything, just like you probably are."

— Scott Nelson

I've got you.

I see you.

I believe you.

What can I do for you?

If discomfort is the price of belonging,
then it's not real belonging.

It's conditional acceptance.

Policies have very real impacts on people.

Neurodivergent, Not Broken stands for policies that center care, dignity, humanity, and protection for those most harmed at the intersections of disability, race, poverty, immigration status, and other marginalized identities.

Solidarity is necessary.
Community care is necessary.

We don't need to be fixed.

We don't need to be optimized.

We don't need to "try harder."

We need a place where we don't
have to explain ourselves.

Somewhere to be understood.
Somewhere to be seen.
Somewhere to be safe.

This started with a simple question:
How do we help each other?

We decided there should be more
community and more support
with real stories.

Neurodivergent and disabled people come
from every culture, race, and language.

We are not a monolith.
Our lives intersect across many identities.

We all bring unique experiences and
wisdom to the table.

Learning in community helps us all.

Community care.

It's horizontal. It's peer-to-peer.
It's relational.

It gives legitimacy to what people have
learned and what they have to contribute.

It doesn't shame people whose
contributions look different from everyone
else's, or those who continually need more
support.

We know we're not the only ones,
and we want you all to know that
you're not the only ones, too.

So this is why we're here.

We want people to feel seen,
heard, and less alone.

Take care of your communities.

Help wherever you have the capacity.

We need each other.

"And literally, if a single person
finds this and gets anything out of
it and says, 'It's not just me.'

That's the peak for me. That's all
I'm hoping for."

— Scott Nelson

Sometimes the bare minimum is all
we're able to give.

That's not a failure. It's called being
human—with a nervous system and
fluctuating capacity.

Capitalism wants you to forget that.

I'm here to remind you: you are not a
machine.

Here's to the ones questioning,
learning, unlearning, repairing,
and growing, even when it's messy.

I'm right here with you.

Sam

About the Author

Sam Nelson is
the creator of
Neurodivergent,
Not Broken.

Her work was built from nearly two decades in relational practice as a hairstylist, her own ADHD, being married to her Autistic husband, raising neurodivergent kids, and caring for her disabled mother.

She offers a way of seeing that centers lived experience as the most important data in the room.

She lives in the Twin Ports — near Lake Superior — with her husband Scott and their two daughters.

website: www.neurodivergentnotbroken.com
substack: @neurodivergentnotbroken